Contents

From nature to transport

How do you get from place to place today? Maybe you travel by bus, bike or car. Designers look for ways to make transport better. Some create safer cars. Others build faster ships. Designers often look to nature for ideas. Copying ideas from nature is called biomimicry.

Fact

The word biomimicry comes from the Greek language. *Bio* means "life". *Mimicry* means "to copy".

...ture

ort

...ature

by Mary Boone

...ntree

...ny — publishers for children

Raintree is an imprint of Capstone Global Library Limited, a company incorporated in England and Wales having its registered office at 264 Banbury Road, Oxford, OX2 7DY – Registered company number: 6695582

www.raintree.co.uk
myorders@raintree.co.uk

Edited by Abby Colich and Jaclyn Jaycox
Designed by Juliette Peters
Picture research by Jo Miller
Production by Katy LaVigne
Printed and bound in India

978 1 4747 8565 5 (hardback)
978 1 4747 8581 5 (paperback)

British Library Cataloguing in Publication Data
A full catalogue record for this book is available from the British Library.

Acknowledgements
b=bottom, l=left, m=middle, r=right, t=top
Alamy; Stockimo/STownyDCC, 19b; AP Images: Vitnija Saldava, 11b; Newscom: Heritage Images/Historica Graphics Collection, 7b, Minden Pictures/Norbert Wu, 17t, Splash/Hammacher-Schlemmer, 15b; Shutterstock: Chaosamran_Studio, 5, frank60, 1m, 13t, iofoto, 7t, Kjeld Friis, 11t, lOvE lOvE, 13b, Monika Wieland Shields, 1l, 15t, RAJU SONI, 1r, 9t, Sean Pavone, Cover, StockStudio, 17b, tackune, 9b, VanderWolf Images, 21b, wildestanimal, 21t, Yann hubert, 19t
Design Elements: Shutterstock: Zubada
Every effort has been made to contact copyright holders of material reproduced in this book. Any omissions will be rectified in subsequent printings if notice is given to the publisher.

It's a bird! It's a plane!

Two brothers called Orville and Wilbur Wright studied birds for a long time. Birds change the shape of their wings as they fly. This lets them turn and change speed. The Wright brothers changed the shape of the wings of their plane. This allowed the plane to move better. In 1903 they built and flew the world's first powered aeroplane.

The Wright brothers' aeroplane in 1903

Trying to fly

The Wright brothers were not the first people to study birds. More than 500 years ago, Leonardo da Vinci sketched flying machines based on birds. His flying machines did not work. However, his ideas inspired others.

Bird to bullet train

Japan's bullet trains are very fast. At first, the train's nose caused a loud crashing sound when it came out of tunnels. A bird-watcher fixed the problem. He saw a kingfisher dive into the water quietly. It didn't even make a splash. The train got a new design. It now looks more like a kingfisher's beak. It is much quieter.

---

species a group of animals with similar features that are capable of reproducing with one another

Fact

About 90 **species** of kingfishers live all over the world. Most live near rivers and lakes. They have long bills. Their feathers are bright colours.

A robot with flippers

Sea turtles use four flippers to swim. They can turn in on the spot and **tread water**. Designers have created a robot that moves in the same way. Like the turtle, the U-CAT robot has four flippers. The flippers paddle in different directions and at different speeds. The robot explores underwater shipwrecks.

---

tread water to float upright in deep water by moving the arms and legs

Researchers tested the U-CAT robot in an aquarium.

Ant trails to delivery lorries

Ants carry food to their nests. They leave behind a substance that marks their paths. The best paths get a build-up of this substance. It lets other ants know the best routes. Delivery lorries have used this method. Computers keep track of all routes travelled. After many deliveries, the computers know the best routes.

Able ants

Ants have a lot to teach people. They can quickly dig tunnels in all kinds of soil. Scientists are studying how. They hope their findings will help them make new robots. The robots would dig tunnels during search-and-rescue missions.

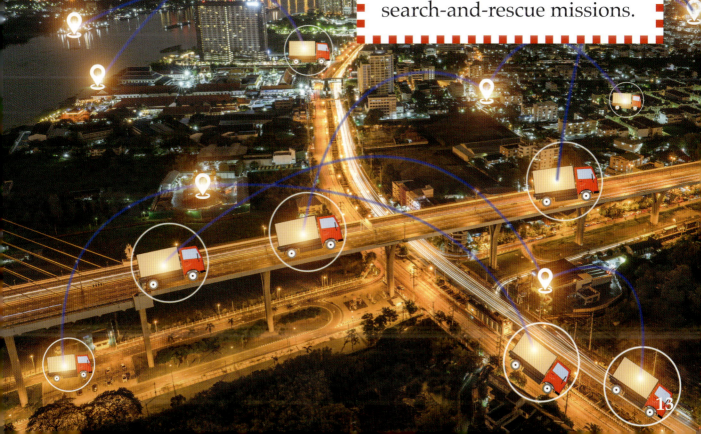

A killer whale submarine

Killer whales jump out of the water. They make a huge splash. This is called **breaching**. They then go back underwater. This is called **submerging**. Designers have created a submarine that looks and moves like a killer whale. Its driver can move the sub's "fins". This allows it to move easily both above and below the water.

breach to jump out of the water

submerge to push below the surface of the water

Fact

Killer whales are not actually whales. They are the largest members of the dolphin family. They are also called orcas.

Speedy bubbles

Emperor penguins can swim fast in cold water. Their feathers release tiny bubbles as they move. The bubbles help them to rise out of the water. This has inspired ship builders. New ships release air bubbles from underneath. These bubbles save energy. They help ships to travel faster.

Fact

Faster ships aren't the only thing penguins have inspired. Designers are considering swimsuits that release bubbles like a penguin's feathers.

Whale fins to bike rims

Zipp is a company that makes racing bikes. It wanted to find a way to make bikes faster. Designers studied a humpback whale's **pectoral fins**. The fins have lumps called **tubercles**. They help the whale to move through the water more easily. Zipp created bike wheels that work like the whale's fins.

pectoral fin fin found on each side of a fish or whale, just behind the head

tubercle small growth or lump on a plant or animal

tubercles

Zipp bike wheels have lumpy rims. This helps the bike move more easily through the wind.

Sailfish to sports cars

Designers at McLaren Automotive started to design a new car. They studied sailfish. These fish travel fast. The fish's scales create tiny pockets of air. Designers copied that design to make the engine for their P1 **hypercar**. More air can flow to the engine. It makes the car faster.

---

hypercar luxury, high-performing sports car

Fact

Sailfish are the fastest fish in the world. They can swim as fast as a car driving on a motorway.

Glossary

breach to jump out of the water

hypercar luxury, high-performing sports car

pectoral fin fin found on each side of a fish or whale, just behind the head

species group of animals with similar features that are capable of reproducing with one another

submerge to push below the surface of the water

tread to float upright in deep water by moving the arms and legs

tubercle small growth or lump on a plant or animal

Find out more

Kingfishers to Bullet Trains (Tech from Nature), Jennifer Colby (Cherry Lake, 2019)

Transport (Building the World), Paul Mason (Wayland, 2019)

Transportation Technology (Designed by Nature), Wendy Lanier (Weigl, 2019)

Websites

BrainPOP: robots
www.brainpop.com / technology / computerscience / robots /

Everyday mysteries: biomimicry for kids
www.loc.gov / rr / scitech / mysteries / biomimicry.html

Learn about how to plan and design with BBC Bitesize
www.bbc.co.uk / bitesize / subjects / zyr9wmn

Comprehension questions

1. Study the photo of the birds on page 7. Can you see how their wings change shape as they fly?

2. Reread page 10. Why do you think a robot that moves like a turtle is good for exploring shipwrecks?

3. Reread page 14. Ask an adult to help you research more about submarines. How is this submarine different from other submarine inventions?

Index